joan cofrancesco

authorHOUSE®

AuthorHouse™
1663 Liberty Drive
Bloomington, IN 47403
www.authorhouse.com
Phone: 1 (800) 839-8640

Published by AuthorHouse 02/01/2018

ISBN: 978-1-5462-2767-0 (sc)
ISBN: 978-1-5462-2795-3 (e)

Print information available on the last page.

Any people depicted in stock imagery provided by Thinkstock are models, and such images are being used for illustrative purposes only. Certain stock imagery © Thinkstock.

This book is printed on acid-free paper.

Because of the dynamic nature of the Internet, any web addresses or links contained in this book may have changed since publication and may no longer be valid. The views expressed in this work are solely those of the author and do not necessarily reflect the views of the publisher, and the publisher hereby disclaims any responsibility for them.

"There's nothing holy about writing but it is the greatest drunken enchantment that I know of."

—Charles Bukowski

from syracuse to nyc
the long train ride chugs
beneath the december moon

let's cuddle
under my cat quilt
we can
stack
wood
later

there is a little bit
of a lot of different poets in me
like garlic salt
with parsley and basil

balthus
loved
his cats &
prepubescent girls
i love sax
& biking through
the dunes
of the cape—
that's life

high noon—
stout to drink
pot to smoke
and retired

nodding off
to basho
beach campfire almost out

alone on christmas
eating a
peanut butter &
jelly sandwich
drinking a beer
feeling like
an ancient dynasty poem

snow on tombstones
cathedral bells ring

sax seduction sanborn
sex hot fudge sunday

early morning beach
dog walkers
man filming birds
one bright orange towel
left in the dunes

i wake up
drink coffee
eat o'hara
lunch poems again

so i wind up
in the cadaver lab
with intestines spleens bones
and formaldehyde stink

FRANK O'HARA DIED
poem for vincent katz july 1967

he was a poet he had lots of friends
i was one of his friends he had some cats

one night with you
instead i spent
eternity wondering
what
it would have been
like

it's almost high noon
on a monday of early may
and all i can think about is
drowning guns

the grey wolf sleeps
under my bed
every night
snoring
sometimes
when
my hand
slithers down
i can feel
his fur

moonlight in the window
lavender scent
from the hot bathtub—
i don't need to be saved

my orange cat
with one ear missing
i call vinnie

her red mg
was always
in the garage

drinking turkish coffee
listening to lennon
then having sex
on the road

in an alternative universe
i have published all your best poems
under my name

crickets
chirping all night
i chant
a cold mountain poem

i get distracted very easily these days:
daffodils, imperial stout, catbirds, etc.

breakfast
i am hypnotized
wind moving the pines
cats stretching

a life with books
cats
a small garden

movie
dinner
a joint
wine
a bath together

i want to climb into
a schwitters assemblage

among the girl faces
tram tickets
cards &
newspaper clips

sunday morning
staring at
your naked
thigh—
religion

my book of poems
arrived 2 days ago
the sea too is calm

every time i open me
bookmarks fall out
and i lose my place

you live in sante fe
with your cat
wolfgang
and your music
wearing those nine-dollar
red converse sneakers

like duchamp
i look for the
miraculous
in everything—
hayden
rocks
urinals

the old buddhist in me
chants. green
norwegian furs
covered with snow
i glisten. beyond
is nowhere i want to go.

wcw

poet
doctor

man
dancing
around his living room

after shoveling
i come in

my body is warm

as vivaldi
on my earphones

in florence
the uffi museum
it was that
spotted dalmation dog
sitting in the doorway
of a store
trying to paw
a fly that
got my attention

a row of small
green and white
cottages
i know i'm almost there

horndog

being 20
horny
& creative
that's going
three
for three

listening to beethoven
piano sonata, no.31
in a flat major opus 110
second movement
when he suddenly jumps to jazz

at the casino
people entranced
by flashing colored
lights—
night of
the living dead

irony—
love inspires me
and blocks my poetry

white cat
on black satin
sheets
red wine

the problem with asking an artist
to look at your stuff
is that he doesn't believe in the 8th commandment

the moon on
the cats head
from the bathroom
window
above
as she drinks
water from
the dripping
faucet

prowling
the metro
in paris
looking for ezra's
petals

as i rake leaves
my orange cat watches
from the window

the ocean
eats a fat woman
like a slice of pizza

when you get old
it's hard to concentrate
you want to be diffuse

shakespeare & company bookstore

black
cat asleep
on the Beats
in a paris bookstore

the nameless way

science technology
materialism
listen to your spirit
god's joker
francis of assisi
shakespeare's fools
rabelais
gulliver's travels
alice in wonderland
the cuttings and
pastings of
kurt schwitters

i hunger for the big stuff—
you
and my cat
sitting beside me
in front of the fireplace
on a cold
syracuse night

i am sick of watching
terrorists every nite
on cnn
but there's
nothing else on

humpback whales
lunge their huge
renoir women
bodies above the sea

i have been waiting
for a new poetry
book by bukowski
even though he
is dead

my cat always
lies on my
bookcase
between
proust and
picasso

i sit quietly
watching my candle
ooze and burn

35 years
at the
marcellus
casket factory
i have quite
an imagination

i never used to care
if there were a head
on my beer
as long as there was plenty of body
but now i want foam
on the mustache of my conversations

sometimes when
i think of you
i think of babylon
were you really there

provincetown
under a tree
we eat 69 clams

come lie next to me
it's raining outside and
there's nothing else to do

temple bell
windowful of cats
i have been practicing
out of body travel
floating above my bed

in my dream

i am sitting on a rock at robert bly's farm. all the poets are there. poe and his raven. gertrude checking out my breasts. rimbaud and verlaine are fighting. o'hara is eyeing some young blond poet and you my muse…you are pretty and young and petting one of bly's black barn cats and you are smiling at me and we are still in love.

watching the dance
of the dead
as i drink
my manhattan
cremation will be
next

syracuse snowstorm
i stayed home
from school
i had to figure out
how far
sirius
is from earth

rainy afternoon
we talk about
movies poetry
kierkegaard
cardiology
two childless women
one orange cat

cat sleeping on
a couch
in a bookstore
in new paltz
on a rainy
afternoon

gurdjieff
why are you one
of the few
people who makes sense
to me these days—
carriage
  horse
      driven
       master

the night the lady bowlers came
into dominic's italian restaurant
like they owned the place

i was sitting at the bar
and one of the big ones
asks hey baby

where can a
woman get some action
in this town?

a glass of red wine
one last trisket
its snowing
in syracuse
so what else is new
sunrise on the
bird feeder

coming into town
a row of little white and green cottages
i know i am almost there

to watch you strut
across the bedroom in your black

lace underwear is to see
my life start over

your black cat rubs
against my leg
purring

i was dead
until now

the rainbow
   embroidered
      on your
  faded jean jacket

      is so
          60's
sexy

i waited nervously
as the psychic
turned over the
next card—
death

i turned
my back
on factories
and accounting firms
i turned
my back
on hospitals, schools
and gave up my life
for imaginings

snow

10 below zero
black cat curled
beside me
in front of the woodstove
listening to
the white album

your love
for me
grew less
and less
like the
rivers in a
chinese
painting

in a dingy
used bookstore
in woodstock
i see a black cat
who leads me to
a first edition of brautigan's
please plant this book

black cats
good luck

the ocean is shining
like a sapphire
i sit in a noisy outdoor café
sipping merlot
reading hacker
as the waiter
serves me the head
of john the baptist
on a gold platter

poem to david masello

because you don't love me
i seek refuge
in the poet's corner in
new york's st. john the divine
and read
w.h. auden's lines
incised in stone
from "the more loving one":
"if equal affection cannot be,
let the more loving one be me."

you remind me
of a dekooning woman
come to life—
all teeth
no soul

let's go down
to the beat hotel
hang with
brion
and burroughs
cut up
some
eat some
brownies
poems

he said
"my kid
was playing
on the internet
the next day
i got a
bill
in the mail
for 55.00 dollars
for
zombie
brains"

my time
when urinals
and soupcans
finally make it
into the museum
to hang with
the renoirs

drinking
mimosas
in the morning
in brooklyn
what a great way
to start

from the balcony

imagining her
muscular thighs
under her jeans
looking down at
her long brown hair
as she mounts her baby blue
datsun 280z

there is nothing better
than walking into
a used bookstore
in brooklyn
on a rainy afternoon

and finding
a black cat sleeping
beside a first edition
of
apollinaire

watching a cat
watching a
muskrat
at the
erie canal—
sex and death

balthus
loves cats
and pre-pubescent girls
i love sanborn's
saxophone &
biking through
the dunes
of the cape—

the world goes on

somewhere else

watching a seagull
on mcmillan's
wharf
a sunset on
herring cove
sea grass moving
in the wind
guitar player
in the square
a kid eating ice cream
a drag queen
rollerblading by

the waves
salty and cold
then their undercurrent

orion's belt
above us
as we sit
by the firepit
drinking
white wine

riding the d
train
to brooklyn museum
to see
basquait

who used to
spray graffiti
on these
trains

upstate winter 2015

reading paul celan
by the fire
my black cat beside me
i hear the cold wind
blowing
it's been a long winter

she's the type
of woman
who as a kid
would rather play
monopoly
than draw—

today it's all
urinals and soupcans
i won't ever be able
to look at renoir
the same

mapplethorpe
flowers
dicks
and patty smith
while old cape cod
plays
in an antique store
on commercial street

my beat lover
for breakfast
wearing only
a black beret

i love to watch her
take a bath
skylight sunshine
on her skin

the key to writing
poetry
is to grab
the divine
between your teeth
and then to
spit it out
onto the paper

your legs are catalogued
in my mind
somewhere
between
brando's arms
and
marilyn's breasts

i want to be driven
van gogh in arles
picasso in paris
haring when he knew
his time was short
i want to live

baking cookies
thinking of
sylvia plath